COURT JESTING

ACKNOWLEDGMENTS

The author and publishers wish to thank all those who have given permission to reproduce copyright material: Associated Newspapers Group Ltd, The Sunday Telegraph, Express Newspapers Ltd, The Observer, Syndication International, John Murray (Publishers) Ltd, Private Eye and particular thanks to Punch magazine. John Kent gave kind permission for his drawing, 'Maggie Rules O.K.', to be used, and Wally Fawkes (Trog) lent an invaluable number of his original drawings. Strenuous efforts were made to trace date and place of first publication of all the drawings in this book, and apologies are made that some proved too elusive.

COURT JESTING

Highlights from the Queen's Life
Through the Eyes of Her Cartoonists

Compiled and Presented by
MARGARET HOWARD

 Robson Books

Designed by Harold King
Researched by Lucy Geidt

First published in Great Britain in 1986 by Robson Books Ltd.,
Bolsover House, 5-6 Clipstone Street, London W1P 7EB.

British Library Cataloguing in Publication Data

Court jesting.
  1. English wit and humor, Pictorial
  2. Great Britain ——— Kings and rulers ———
Caricatures and cartoons
  I. Howard, Margaret
  741.5'942 NC1476

ISBN 0-86051-384-X

Printed in Great Britain by The Garden City Press, Letchworth.

CONTENTS

Punch, June 4 1980

'I've sometimes wondered whether we couldn't perhaps be a little less exemplary.'

INTRODUCTION

It's not easy to laugh at the Queen. Her conscientious, hard-working image is admirable rather than risible, the more so as she's now reached the age at which woman are expected to retire. Her failings are not so instantly obvious as those of her ancestors like George IV, who was viciously lampooned in his day.

At the beginning of her public life as Princess Elizabeth, the heir apparent, artists seemed to see her as a creature in a fairy story. No hint of criticism crept in. It was a much more forelock-touching generation than the generation of today, and her father and mother had gained the respect of the country during the war. When peacetime came, a kind of innocent euphoria took over the national consciousness and found a focus in the young princess.

Her betrothal and marriage were followed with passionate interest, as was her coronation. The years following the Second World War were pretty bleak, but the splash of extravagance on Hartnell's magnificent embroidered gowns for these two historic occasions excited enthusiasm rather than envy. I have included the drawings and descriptions as a matter of historical interest.

Looking back over some of the cartoons of the Queen during her reign, I see that few have been cruel, most are affectionate. There are those who have tried to reduce her stature by calling her names like Betty Windsor. *Private Eye* has a go at her by dubbing her Brenda, the ultimate none-name of the middle class. Spitting Image puts her television puppet in headscarf and crown together. None of them have managed to diminish her stern dignity and sense of purpose. Beneath it all, I would like to think – and I have heard it said – that the Queen has a sense of humour.

This book is designed as an affectionate tribute to Her Majesty. Her cartoonists, on the whole, do not seek to knock. Like me, I suspect, they are happiest offering her loyal greetings.

Margaret Howard
London, February 1986

PRINCESS ELIZABETH

At the age of twenty-one the Queen, then Princess Elizabeth, dedicated her life to her future subjects. She was on a tour of South Africa, at that time a member of the Commonwealth. In her coming-of-age broadcast from Government House she said, 'I declare before you all that my whole life, whether it be long or short, shall be devoted to your service and the service of the great Imperial Commonwealth to which we all belong.'

Mr Punch took off his hat to her. It was clearly not seen as an occasion for satire. Instead, this whimsical drawing foreshadowing her future role was composed by the illustrator of *Winnie-the-Pooh*, E.H. Shepard.

Punch, April 23 1947

Birthday greetings

A future Queen needed a future consort, and before the year was out Buckingham Palace announced the betrothal of Her Royal Highness the Princess Elizabeth to Lieutenant Philip Mountbatten, a naval officer and member of the Greek royal family. The country was euphoric. 'All the nice girls love a sailor', they sang and E.H. Shepard in *Punch* gave visual expression to the naval motif.

Punch, July 16 1947

Betrothed

It was a time of austerity. In the aftermath of the Second World War, you still needed coupons to buy clothes. In common with other brides, Princess Elizabeth was allowed extra coupons. In her case an extra hundred. Her six bridesmaids got an extra twenty-three coupons each. However, gifts from all over the world of silk, brocade and muslin fabrics rolled in, and Queen Elizabeth and Queen Mary had been squirrelling bits away against the day.

The royal dress designer, Norman Hartnell, excelled himself with a gown of pure silk duchesse satin embroidered with garlands of flowers, including York roses and wheat ears of seed pearls and tiny glistening crystals. Twenty-five embroideresses worked on the dresses for the bride and bridesmaids for two months. The tulle veil was held in place by a pearl and diamond tiara, and the Princess carried a bouquet of white orchids.

Drawing by
PEMBERTON

The Wedding Dress

News Chronicle, November 20 1947

The bride's 'going away' outfit consisted of a dress of 'love in a mist' blue crepe with a cross-over bodice and a coat of blue velour. A bonnet of blue felt with an ostrich pom-pom completed the ensemble.

Meanwhile, back at Westminster, Low hoped that the national mood of sweetness and light would spread to the old political rivals, Clement Attlee and Winston Churchill.

The Standard, November 21 1947

After the great day – the spread of romance

It was a chill November day in 1947 when they got married, but the pageantry warmed the hearts of a war-torn people. Fired with the spirit of romanticism, E.H. Shepard imagined the long line of people linking the Princess to the first Elizabeth – and showed them drawing her wedding carriage into a second Elizabethan age.

Punch, November 19 1947

A day of history

On the day of the wedding the King created Philip Duke of Edinburgh, and he set about finding a niche for himself in the royal family.

His interest in sailing, polo and flying and his pet concern of fostering activities for the young inspired Illingworth to this sentimental picture for *Punch*.

Punch Coronation Number, May 20 1953

Royal right hand

Almost exactly a year after the royal wedding, on November 14 1948 Buckingham Palace announced, 'The Princess Elizabeth, Duchess of Edinburgh was safely delivered of a Prince at 9.14 pm today. Her Royal Highness and her son are both doing well.'

The *Daily Mail*'s cartoonist had this rather less formal and factual view of the event.

Daily Mail, November 15 1948

'I circled twice for the benefit of the crowd before making a perfect two-point landing'

Two years later a Princess was born. 'We are so lucky, Philip and I,' the future Queen said. As years of royal childhood went by, *Punch* saw the whole thing as a fairytale.

Royal road to the future

Leaving the children behind, the royal couple left on a foreign tour. While they were on a wildlife observation trip in Kenya, the news was brought to them that the King had died. The new Queen, only twenty-five years old, hastened home to be met by her Prime Minister, Winston Churchill, and a people who somehow hoped that she personified the beginning of a golden age, the reign of a second Elizabeth.

Sunday Express, February 10 1952

'Take the torch. Let our peoples see what another Elizabeth can do.'

CJ-2

George VI had been much loved. Illingworth had a classical figure carve his epitaph in a tablet of stone.

GEORGE VI
REGN.
1936 – 1952

COURAGE

ENDURANCE

KINDLINESS

DEVOTION

Punch, 1952

After a period of mourning the coronation was to take place. A new era had begun.

CORONATION

Punch, May 20 1953

Coronation fever gripped the land . . .

Highland games

'If he plants "The Second", in you all go and get scratching.'

The British Mount Everest Expedition conquered the world's highest peak in time for the big day, and Illingworth imagined that even the murky deep had prepared a loyal gesture.

The Mall leading up to Buckingham Palace was decked overall, and every village and town throughout the Commonwealth put out their flags.

Punch, May 27 1953

The East End Gets Ready

London from the East End to the West End was in a right royal good humour.

Punch and the Monarchy, 1952

The West End Celebrates

Punch and the Monarchy, 1953

There were pageants and fêtes and firework displays – explosions of delight from a small squib . . .

Punch and the Monarchy, 1953

'. . . not forgetting Mr Jackson, who gave invaluable help with the fireworks.'

... to a big bang.

Punch Coronation Number, May 20 1953

Rising to the Occasion
The Director of Harwell lets off a small firework

Members of the peerage shook the mothballs out of their ermine, donned their coronets and headed for their places in Westminster Abbey.

POCKET CARTOON
by OSBERT LANCASTER

Daily Express, June 2 1953

'Darling, what would you say if I were to tell you I'd left the tickets in the cloakroom at the Four Hundred?'

Punch and the Monarchy, 1953

The dress for the central small figure of the Queen took a little longer to prepare. Norman Hartnell was asked to submit designs in October 1952 for the June 1953 deadline. His brief was to create something grand and symbolic. He decided that the dress should bear the emblems of Great Britain. The Queen added that she would also like to include the emblems of the Commonwealth.

Six girls worked on the embroidery. The leek of Wales was picked out in green and studded with pearls and diamonds, the shamrock of Ireland in emeralds and diamonds, and the thistle of Scotland in amethysts. Around the hem were the maple leaf of Canada, mimosa for Australia, fern for New Zealand, all woven around the Tudor rose.

EXCLUSIVE!

~~~ the Daily Express artist, is the only man — apart from designer Norman Hartnell—who has seen the gowns the Queen and the Royal Family wear today. It is from his drawings, and Hartnell's sketches, that the world's Press has now learned the greatest-ever fashion secret.

Daily Express, June 2 1953

There were those, notably in the Labour Party, who disapproved of such an ostentatious display of wealth.

IF THE BEVANITES RAN THE CORONATION . . .

Daily Express, June 1 1953

But nothing, not even the overnight rain, could dampen the enthusiasm of the crowds who had come to line the processional route. They spent the night out under oilskins and groundsheets, vacuum flasks and sardine sandwiches. The determination to get a good view was phenomenal.

Daily Mirror, June 2 1953

'Did you hear that?
It cheered!'

Our newly crowned and annointed Queen set off on a tour of her realm or, at least, she went to Scotland and Wales. England was slightly miffed at being left out, although a lot of the activities centred on London. There was a service of thanksgiving at St

Paul's, a lunch at the Guildhall, and she dropped in on the Test Match at Lord's where, in honour of coronation year, England won the Ashes.

Fifty-three thousand ex-servicemen paraded in Hyde Park and Her Majesty reviewed them from the back of a jeep. Then there was the Spithead Review of the Fleet, a royal review of the RAF at Odiham. Not to mention Royal Ascot and a visit to the boys of Eton College. All in all, the new Queen and her consort must have been relieved to get to their Scottish retreat, Balmoral, in time for the Queen Mother's birthday on August 4.

Punch, August 5 1953

Well-earned rest
The Queen is due at Balmoral to-day

ROYAL TOURS

But they didn't rest long. Soon they were off again. The first Commonwealth Tour of the reign began on November 24 1953 and ended in May 1954 after taking in Bermuda, Jamaica, Fiji, Tonga, New Zealand, Australia, Cocos Isles, Ceylon, Aden, Uganda, Libya, Malta and Gilbraltar. Perhaps the first Elizabeth would not have approved.

'My more spirited subjects used to globetrot while I stayed at home. What are all your Sir Walter Raleighs doing?'

Royal Tours became a feature of the reign and, over the years, we have seen the Queen setting off countless times with carefully-prepared wardrobes to suit all climates and eventualities, ready to wave the royal wave and watch endless displays of national dance and custom.

'Honestly, Norman, I much preferred your collection for my American Tour.'

Standard, 1977

CJ-3

'You must excuse my equerry – it's his first Royal Tour to New Zealand!'

Standard, 1977

34

I imagine that there is not much time for sending postcards home on a Royal Tour but here Stan McMurtry imagines the Queen taking a moment to write up her diary under a Pacific palm tree, while technology takes over her official business.

Punch, June 20 1977

Ever since her wet coronation on June 2 1953 'Queen's weather' has come to mean rain. But never was there such a deluge as when the Queen and Prince Philip went to California, the 'sunshine state', in 1983. The cartoonists had a field day.

The Standard, March 3 1983

'. . . And here she comes now folks, wearing an off-the-shoulder chiffon gown with yards of pink tulle, the Dook is doing the backstroke!'

But all the same she was given a warm and homely welcome.

'When you've settled in, folks, mosey on over to the bunkhouse where Nancy's rustled up some beans, bacon and grits.'

Daily Mail, March I 1983

The royal children had by now been introduced to the rigours of flying the flag overseas. In 1977, for instance, Prince Charles was in Canada. On a five-day visit to the province of Alberta he took part in a centenary re-enactment of an ancient Indian treaty. He became an honorary Kinai Indian chieftain named Red Crow for the occasion, and submitted to being decorated with eagle feathers and warpaint. He joined in the sacred Sun Dance Circle and took part in Grass Dance, Moon Dance and Chicken Dance.

To show that the tomahawk was well and truly buried (the hundred-year-old treaty had, after all, annexed to the Crown Indian prairies in Southern Alberta belonging to the Blackfoot, Blood, Peigan, Sarcee and Stony Indian tribes), Prince Charles sat down to smoke a pipe of peace. There was much speculation at the time about whom the heir to the throne would marry. Some predicted that he would choose a bride from the Commonwealth.

'I trust H R H Red Crow realises that last little ceremonial puff made my daughter the future Queen of England.'

Sunday Express, July 10 1977

PLANES AND BOATS AND TRAINS

'I don't know that they've any right to expect a Royal Tour
from a Bicycle Monarchy.'

Punch, November 19 1969

A lot of the Queen's getting about is done in this country by royal train. It was, after all, supposed to be quicker by rail.

'Five beakers of champagne – and Princess Margaret would like a pork pie with the cellophane taken off.'

Pardon me. Boy. is that the House of Windsor Choo-choo?

GEOFFREY DICKINSON has been spotting the new Royal Train

'Relax! – departure's delayed for an hour, the Duke has just found out they can get a cheap-day return after 9.30.'

'Well sir, since Manchester United were at home today that only leaves. . .'

'What are they like on Wagner's *Ring*? – there's a points failure at Haywards Heath.'

Punch, April 6 1977

Later British Rail's slogan became 'We're getting there'. Getting there more slowly than ever, might have been the Queen's comment when she travelled on the 7.50 from Kings Lynn to Liverpool Street and it broke down eight times and arrived forty-three minutes late. All power from the traction motors had to be directed to the faltering engine so there was no heating in the carriages. On top of that the door to the breakfast car was found to be locked and no-one had a key.

For journeys to further-flung places there is always the royal yacht, but that is an expensive item and from time to time there have been rumours that it might have to go.

And when it came to planes, Prince Philip has been known to complain that he sometimes feels he is living at either end of a runway at Heathrow with heavy aircraft noise over both Buckingham Palace and Windsor Castle.

9d

Concorde

Observer, December 1968

Concorde is the chief offender when it comes to noise, and when the aircraft featured on a New Year commemoration stamp at the end of 1968 Trog suggested this new variant on the sovereign's head.

SAIL THE FLAG

When the Royal Family heard of Government worries about the cost of the Britannia refit, they organised a Royal fund-raising cruise. MAHOOD bought a ticket

PMs AND PARLIAMENTARY MATTERS

Upholding the constitutional monarchy has always been a tricky balancing act. Here, in Trog's drawing with seven of her Prime Ministers in the ring the Queen is, undoubtedly, the star of the show.

THE ROYAL CIRCUS

During the 1974 election campaign a major theme was 'Who Rules Britain?' Was it the unions, the government or who?

The expenses of the royal household and the amount allocated to the Civil List are occasional bones of contention. Will it ever come to this?

'My husband and I . . .'

The Observer, 16 February 1975

The most persistent and outspoken critic of royal expenditure has been the Labour Member for Fife Central, William Hamilton. Emmwood had him clapped in the Tower for his pains.

'Her Majesty has nothing against you personally, Mister Hamilton, but for your own protection thinks it best . . .'

The Labour leader, however, was more respectful.

'Don't feel you need fly back *each day* to report, Prime Minister.'

Could it be that he had something to hide?

'"... and my total earnings for 1973-74 were ..." oh, dear, I seem to have someone's tax forms mixed up with my speech.'

Daily Mail, 1974

By 1979 another election was in the offing. If the Conservatives got in, there would be two leading ladies in the land. Who would bow the knee to whom?

Observer, 1979

MAGGIE RULES OK BY JOHN KENT

Private Eye, November 15 1986

AT WORK

Well, let's say they both have a job to do.

For Her Majesty it may be wielding the sword over the bow-tied Robin Day.

Private Eye, February 27 1981

Though Honeysett envisaged a more unusual way of bestowing honours.

HONEYSETT

Private Eye, February 18 1977

Wherever she goes security is ever-present.

And loyal subjects sit in their bungalows and dream about the Queen. This cartoon by Mahood arose from an advertisement offering a house for sale to whites only. He dreamt up the ultimate in discrimination.

'I'm not certain, but I think this may be one for
the Sex Discrimination Board!'

To ease the royal lot, Maddocks in *Private Eye* invented reviewing the troops by roller skate. It didn't catch on. What a pity!

Private Eye, August I I 1980

But the Queen, making no concessions to aching royal feet, went walkabout down under.

'Follow that bicycle!'

'Showing off a bit today. Doesn't usually wear her fur to go and buy chips!'

THE QUEEN MEETS SAM HINCHCLIFFE

After the Royal Family's remarkably successful impromptu chats with the Aussie crowds, will they try it on here? Your guess is as good as Bill Tidy's.

'The Queen is resting. If you're looking for news, try Princess Margaret at Number 24!'

'From your Nellie's cooking, more like it!'

'...amn kids! Gerrof that flamin' car!'

'Don't worry, luv. You only get grunts from him when he's watching results sequence!'

'We'd love to visit you, luv, but not this year. We're going to Blackpool.'

Punch, April 22 1970

Did the heatwàve of 1976 really provoke this Marie Antoinette-like response?

PRIVATE EYE

No. 383
Friday
20 Aug. '76

20p

WATER SHORTAGE:
Queen's Message

Let them drink Coke!

Whatever went on in the royal mind, the remorseless round of tours – foreign and local – went on. Larry makes this visit look quite fun.

MY FACTORY AND I

Punch, June 29 1977

This is Mahood indulging in a bit of stargazing for *Punch*.

Mahood 1986 and all that

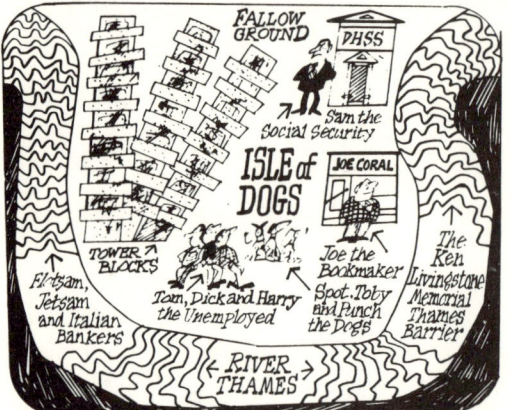

The BBC is planning for 1986 a new Domesday Book containing
two million pages of pictures, facts, figures and maps about life in Britain today.

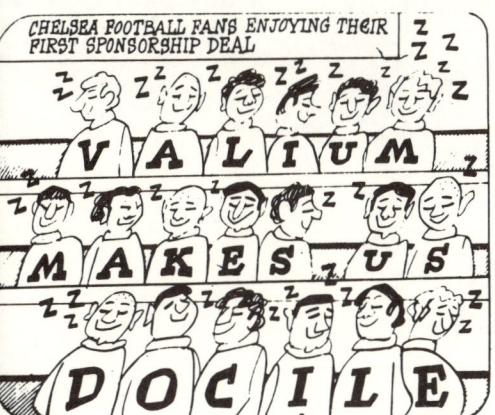

CHELSEA FOOTBALL FANS ENJOYING THEIR FIRST SPONSORSHIP DEAL

VALIUM MAKES US DOCILE

GROUP THERAPY AT THE THATCHER PSYCHIATRIC WARD FOR DISAPPOINTED APPLICANTS FOR BRITISH TELECOM SHARES

3,000,000 CITIZENS PATIENTLY WAITING FOR A TORY GOOD SAMARITAN TO APPEAR

UNEMPLOYMENT OFFICE

QUEUE HERE

THE GOVERNMENT SOLVES THE RACIAL PREJUDICE PROBLEM

FREE TO EVERYONE ROSE-TINTED SPECTACLES

SHOP STEWARDS ATTENDING A MASS MEETING TO VOTE ON STRIKE ACTION

AUSTIN ROVER →

THE DAILY MIRROR OFFERS THE ULTIMATE BINGO PRIZE

WIN YOUR OWN EXCITING DYNAMIC BILLIONAIRE IN THE Mirror

Punch, November 21 1984

'But it's the only sort of work I know.'

Trog painted a picture of a hard-working partnership at Buckingham Palace, but Honeysett saw his fictional monarch as being all part of Britain on the Fiddle.

Observer. 1971

Punch, April 21 1982

'I'm going to sneak away early – will you clock me off?'

AT HOME

LARRY

My Christmas and I...

Even the most hard-working families must take a break some time. What better than an occasion for the whole family to get together and celebrate?

Punch, December 7 1983

Here are some more cartoonist's glimpses into the home life of our own dear Queen.

'Just the "Morning Star" today – it's the only one with nothing in it to upset Her.'

Punch, December 10 1980

'Gone to luncheon – back in half-an-hour.'

Punch, 28 September 1983

'The lowest common denominator – that's all they ever aim at! What about me for a change?'

Private Eye, October 1 1976

It happens in every family. Was it Prince Charles who bowled a cricket ball through the windows of Buckingham Palace in 1957? It was the year he had his tonsils and adenoids out and he started at his prep school, Cheam.

'If you are the State, we'd better have him educated privately!'

'There's this about my old school – that careers master certainly knew his stuff!'

By 1973 the two eldest children were grown up. Princess Anne announced her intention to marry Captain Mark Phillips, an army officer and horseman of some repute. The family had a royal wedding on its hands once again. The big day was November 14 1973.

Every year the Queen is At Home to many hundreds of her subjects and overseas visitors, who are invited to take tea on the camomile lawns at Buckingham Palace.

Honeysett:
UP FOR THE CUPPA

'They don't usually arrive until after the pubs shut.'

'I mean, where does anyone get decent staff these days?'

'I know we've got an invitation, but I want to see i my security chappies are on the ball.'

'I hope we don't have to kneel.'

'No ashtrays.'

'I don't want to embarrass Her Majesty by wearing the same dress so I've taken it off.'

'It's all right – she says they can manage the clearing-up.'

Punch, August 10 1983

HORSES AND SPORT

The family interest in horses is well known.

'Who won the two-thirty at Epsom?'

They patronise other sports also, and are frequently at the F.A. Cup Final. In 1958, however, the Duke of Edinburgh had to go to Wembley on his own. The Queen had a bad cold and stayed at home, which inspired Belsky's speculative spiv.

'Psst! How about a fiver for the Queen's Cup Final ticket?'

A highlight of the racing calender is Royal Ascot. Some people resent the display of wealth that it involves, so Honeysett invented a new version on the old theme.

AUSTERITY ASCOT

'I don't think I'll back the Queen's horse this time.'

'More Tizer, your ladyship?'

'Let me introduce you to the Duchess of Blackpool.'

Punch, June 15 1977

Mahood saw the Queen as a tipster in quite another sport.

'Judges are not elected but are appointed by the Queen. Luckily for our judicial system she has plenty of experience in picking winners.'

COMMAND PERFORMANCES

The Queen's presence is also required at annual command performances on stage and screen.

Punch, February 26 1969

'Right then. Royal Command Performance, seven-thirty, Tuesday. I'll meet you outside.'

'A GENTLEMAN CALLED...' by Giles

Sunday Express, October 1952

'A gentleman called and sold me two seats for tomorrow's Royal Film Performance – front row right next to Charlie Chaplin and the Queen.'

Observer, 1971

'On your toes everybody – here comes Mr Delfont!'

It must all be very tiring . . .

'Well, it has been an exhausting year!'

Punch, December 17 1977

Time, in fact, for a holiday.

Woman's Own, August 17 1985

Drop everything and take our You're-As-Young-As-You-Feel break to the Scottish Highlands – the fun starts the minute you leave on our air-conditioned coach. We know you'll enjoy this friendly, informal holiday and the good home-cooking offered at all our stop-over Guest Houses. To help you chum up with your fellow-travellers we've organised a wide choice of entertainments – bingo, whist drives, highland games. PETS ALLOWED.

JUBILEE

1977 was the 25th anniversary of the Queen's accession. It was decided to celebrate the Jubilee in joyous style.

'You are supposed to hold your street party in your street not hers.'

The occasion merited a Jubilee Hymn from the Poet Laureate. These lines written without benefit of butt of sack appeared in *Private Eye*.

POETRY CORNER

To Our Lovely Young Queen On The Happy Occasion Of Her Jubilee

Lines specially written by Alfred, Lord Betjeperson.

Ding dong, ding dong
Go the bells of London town
Is it really that long
Since she put on the Crown?

Look at the daffs under the trees
Golden for the jubilee
Their trumpets waving in the breeze
Bring a thrill to you and me.

CHORUS:

Dear old Brenda, don't you love her?
She's the girl for me all right
And what about the old Queen Mother
She's a nice old stick . . . te-tum-te-tum

(Can you fill in the rest – I've got to dash now. Pip, pip. J.B.)

JUBILEE SOUVENIR

25

UNAUTHORISED

KenTaylor

Punch, April 6 1977

Royal souvenirs abounded and *Punch* invented some more.

They're Crumbling the Cookies at Buckingham Palace

— and Handelsman Creative Hacks Ltd have already prepared their campaigns for Jubilee Year. Let's run them up the Royal Family and see if anyone changes the guard

COME TO BRITAIN

Watch the picturesque natives at their traditional pastimes

...and don't miss the fabulous stockbroker belt!

BRITIS
TOURI
BOARD

The whisky with 25 years of experience...

LIZ & PHIL

FROM GLENMILLER DISTILLERIES

Dignified but approachable, stately yet skilled at small talk. It's almost balmoral.

"Don't take a pill — take Liz & Phil."

By appointment to STEVE McQueen

It's Jubilee Year — so feed *your* corgi

SHOW JUMPER CHUNKS

as ridden by royalty!

Yum!

 Punch, April 6 1977

The Jubilee inspired poetic memories, too, in other even more unlikely breasts.

'Twenty-five years ago! When I told you you looked like the Duke . . . and you called me your princess. Remember?'

Sunday Express, February 6 1977

And it provided an excuse for a knees-up.

Punch, April 6 1977

There were flags and street parties everywhere.

Daily Express. June 6 1977

'Damn Joneses – He's wearing a white tie!'

'Started as a Jubilee street party – finished up a Jubilee beacon.'

Daily Mirror, June 7 1977

And the Queen took tea with a family in an ordinary council house, which meant that many noses were put out of joint.

Daily Express, June 8 1977

'Ladies! What would Her Majesty say – just because you say your neighbour's hung on to three of your chairs and she says you've nicked six of her forks.'

'Remember they're for your father's tea so don't go giving them to the Royalty.'

Sunday Express, February 6 1977

Many overseas visitors came for the celebrations, particularly as the Commonwealth Conference was to take place in London shortly afterwards.

Idi Amin, whose reign of terror was at its height in Uganda at the time, wrote to the Commonwealth Secretary General to suggest that as an old friend of the Queen he should be put up at Buckingham Palace.

Sunday Express, April 24 1977

Official proof from Big Daddy's album that he knew the Queen before Prince Philip did.

He was discouraged from attending.

Evening Standard, June 3 1977

'And I haven't invited the Queen!'

'... And in the next carriage we have ...'

Daily Mirror, June 8 1977

Despite what Keith Waite drew, he was not in any Jubilee procession.

INVASION OF PRIVACY

Relations between the Palace and the press sometimes become strained. Paparazzi techniques and long lenses meet with royal rebuke. A pregnant bikini-clad Princess of Wales is strictly for the family album, and not page 3 of the *Sun*.

But for one glorious moment Trog lets the Queen turn the tables.

'I've got these terrific pictures of the Queen being angry about those bikini photos!'

Punch, March 10 1982

Observer, January 8 1984

And Heath saw the Queen taking over the microphone and doing a turn.

Michael Heath

Standard, March 2 1983

'My husband and I, and this'll slay yer . . .!'

As for the BBC. . . . Well, in 1977 they had an anniversary to celebrate as well, and you know what the BBC is like about anniversaries.

Daily Mirror, November 13 1977

'**I sometimes think the BBC are overdoing their anniversary.**'

But then came the most intrusive invader of the Queen's privacy of them all. Her Majesty woke up one morning to find a stranger sitting at the end of her bed.

Fortunately, he was apprehended before he did any harm. Afterwards, security at the Palace was tightened up.

Standard. March 27 1983

'But anybody could say they were the Queen.'

'Haven't you heard? They've let Michael Fagan out.'

The world of Keith Waite

Daily Mirror. January 21 1983

THE FOREIGN VIEW OF THE QUEEN

Though our national institution of the monarchy may be criticised, it's clearly envied sometimes by people in other countries. At the time of the coronation, Americans had their dreams and their frustrations.

A TRAVELLER'S DREAM OF HOME

Daily Express, May 28 1953

'Stop, Elmer, stop! You're dreaming that un-American dream again . . .'

'But Hank, Hank – you mustn't let a little thing like a coronation discourage you!'

What would happen if Her Majesty re-adopted her former colony? Would she take to the razzamataz?

Some of us never pay attention to or think about royalty or anything else, for that matter.

If certain Britons have their way, the royal family might find themselves unemployed. They could emigrate to the United States—starting a Brougham rain. Their chances finding work—and general acceptance of them—would depend on certain attitudes already existing among us, says America's Arnold Roth.

Her Majesty should be forewarned that certain individuals are still angry at her great-great-great-great grandfather and his crowd.

We do desperately need a full-time functionary who would free the President to concentrate all his energies on ruining the nation.

Many fans would bring to the royal presence a kind of dedication which only converts possess.

A modicum of adjustment might be necessary for all concerned.

There are people here who have little respect for anything.

Longed-for thrills could be provided for those of our humble citizens who want for nothing.

Punch, June 24 1970

The present star of the American scene is President Reagan.

He crossed the Atlantic in 1984 to try and find his roots in Ireland, and stopped off in London for the Economic Summit.

His first visit after taking office had been two years earlier. He stayed with the Royal Family at Windsor Castle, where every comfort was laid on for him and his First Lady.

Daily Mail, June 7 1982

'Ain't that nice, Nancy? Her Majesty has given us a room where I can quietly contemplate the US attitude over the Falklands.'

In October 1984 the Queen went to the States on private business. She visited several stud farms in Kentucky to look at stallions to mate with her mares. Kentucky , of course, is famous for more than its horses – the chicken there is said to be 'finger-lickin' good'.

'Ah! Colonel Sanders. Philip often nips out for one of your take-aways!'

Which came first, the chicken or the egg? In New Zealand, on her 1986 tour, the Queen was at the receiving end of a few eggs – thrown at her by disaffected members of the Commonwealth. As usual, the royal nerve was unshaken.

'Thank you Perkins, that will be all – I think we're ready for them tomorrow.'

Daily Mail, February 25 1986

As for France, which sent its own aristocracy to the guillotine, royal watching is a national pastime there. But was the *entente* ever this *cordiale*?

The fact is that Europe has shed sovereigns rather than created them. Our monarchy has survived to inspire us, unite us and, as in these pages I hope, to cheer us up. The institution has severe critics but it looks set to continue – always supposing it wants to.

'Is it really true that one day all this will be mine?'